the key to more miracles in your life

Marilyn & Sarah
MARILYN HICKEY MINISTRIES

mhmin.org

P.O. Box 6598
Englewood, CO 80155-6598

the key to more miracles in your life

Copyright © 2002
by Marilyn Hickey Ministries
P.O. Box 6598
Englewood, Colorado 80155-6598
(303) 770-0400
mhmin.org

ISBN 1-56441-049-8

Printed in the United States of America

Unless otherwise indicated, all Scripture
quotations are taken from the
New King James Version of the Bible.

TABLE OF CONTENTS

Chapter 1
⋖⋗Tap Into a Fresh Anointing From God ⋖⋗

I looked in astonishment at my husband and exclaimed, "Wally! You gave it *all*?" Wally and I have now pastored for more than 40 years. This incident took place when we had just started in ministry. Our congregation was 50 or 60 people, we had very little money, and our car was in terrible shape—it would hardly go. It had taken us long months to scrimp and save a thousand dollars to pay for a "new" used car.

To me, that thousand dollars seemed like all the money in the world. Then, one night in a service held by T.L. and Daisy Osborne—Wally gave every penny of our car money in an offering.

C-A-R Money

As we drove home from the service, Wally explained that God had told him to give our car money. I just couldn't believe it. I was so upset, I was sick to my stomach. I just knew that our old car would die and we would be walking the streets and riding buses. It wasn't that bad, but we did end up driving a borrowed car.

About eight months later, John Osteen stood behind our pulpit for the first time, he pointed at Wally and said, "I see the word *C-A-R* written across your forehead." We had not told John that we needed a car. Then, he received an offering that paid for our next car. Yes, we received a financial harvest for giving, but that wasn't all that gift would accomplish....

Ministry to Nations

Twelve years after Wally gave our car money, I sat in a restaurant across from Daisy Osborne—after I'd been called to my own ministry—and she prophesied that I would take the gospel to the nations of the world (as she and her husband had done). I'm sorry to say, I thought she was crazy—crazy Daisy.

A short time later, when attending a Kenneth Copeland meeting, he prophesied to me exactly the same thing Daisy had said. At the time, I had never ministered outside the country and could hardly believe it would come true, but I was beginning to believe. Now, many years later, I can tell you that I have seen that prophecy fulfilled in my life—and it is still coming to pass.

More recently, I've seen this anointing and call evident in my daughter, Sarah Bowling. That thousand-dollar "seed" sowed many years ago and our partnership with the Osbornes are *still* bringing blessing into our lives and the lives of our children.

Do you see what happened? Yes, God used the principle of "sowing and reaping" to bless us financially, but that wasn't all. Because we had "partnered" with the Osbornes, God used the principle of "ministry partnership" to take my ministry to a higher level. *The anointing upon the Osbornes for international ministry and miracles began to come upon my own ministry.*

Oral Roberts' Smallest Partner

My mother, Mary Sweitzer, was born again and Spirit filled when I was living at home and going to school.

An Anointing of Prosperity...

"*As a result of being a partner with Marilyn and Sarah, my own ministry has begun to prosper. Finances are now coming in to my ministry from the north, south, east, and west. I've truly begun to reap.*"

Emma

As a new Christian, she had a very difficult life. When she tried to witness to me, I had no interest. My father, however, was far worse—he was angry about her "new religion" and her desire to attend church. When she asked him to tithe on his pay, my father hit the ceiling.

He told her she could tithe from her grocery money but he wouldn't give her a penny more. Somehow she found a way to tithe and even became a financial partner with Oral Roberts. She watched him on television and when she was diagnosed with a breast tumor, she touched the TV screen as a point of contact and received a complete healing.

Every month, she faithfully sent her small partner gift. It couldn't have been very much; she had so little money to use. Yet, her small offering was like the widow's mite— God honored and blessed it.

When I became born again, and Wally and I married, we too felt God lead us to become partners with Oral Roberts. We continue to support the Roberts' ministry today. We have been blessed by this partnership in so many ways for so many years, I couldn't begin to tell you about all of them. Yet, let me tell you about two or three that are really important to me.

The First Blessing

The first blessing of being his partner was when Oral Roberts invited me to be the chairperson of the Oral Roberts University Board of Regents. Then ORU conferred upon me an honorary doctor of divinity degree.

Since partnering with Oral Roberts an even more important thing happened—*the anointing for healings and miracles upon the Roberts' ministry began to come upon mine.* I have seen God miraculously heal, literally, thousands of people of every kind of sickness and disease. Recently, at a crusade in Bolivia an entire wheelchair section was nearly emptied.

Also, my daughter, Sarah, attended and graduated from ORU before she joined me in ministry. This partnership with ORU, I believe, also accounts for the incredible success of Word to the World College, my international Bible college.

Now, Sarah is a partner with Richard and Oral Roberts. Would it surprise you to know that Sarah, too, sees healings and miracles everywhere she

A Word From Sarah...
*Getting "hooked on the Book"
is the key to success in life.
Many of our partners write to say they have
developed a new interest in God's Word.
A hunger for the Word is one of the key anointings
upon this ministry, one of the things
that come down on our partners.
Remember when Joshua assumed leadership of
Israel as they entered the Promised Land?
(See Joshua 1:8.) God told Joshua to speak the
Word...meditate on the Word...and do the Word.
God promised that when Joshua did so,
He would make Joshua's "way to prosper,"
and he would have "good success."
You've got to know the Word...
that's the first step!*

ministers? Three of our generations have partnered with the Roberts' healing and Christian education ministry and each has received a great blessing. I would say those are pretty big benefits of ministry partnership— wouldn't you?

Dr. Cho

No doubt you've heard of Dr. David Yonggi Cho, pastor of the world's largest Christian church, the Yoido Full Gospel Church, located in South Korea. Perhaps you've read his amazing story of building a church from a few believers to more than a million people in an overwhelmingly Buddhist nation. Fascinated by the incredible work he was doing for the Lord, Wally and I became partners with Pastor Cho.

What you may not know is that Dr. Cho and his church are tremendously active in international ministry. He holds large crusades all over the world and sends missionaries to the farthest reaches of the earth.

Although I had not yet met Dr. Cho, I felt that God wanted me to be on the board of directors of his Church Growth International Ministries. I knew one minister on his board, and contacted him. He informed me that there were no women on the board and I told him that was good reason for Dr. Cho to invite me to join them. The pastor said he would mention my request at their next meeting.

Dream Fulfilled

Time passed and when I contacted this pastor again, he said they had considered my request and decided they didn't need me on the board. Was I disappointed? Yes. Was I discouraged? Yes. Did I give up? NO!

I refused to give up the dream God had put in my heart...and I absolutely refused to be offended. I continued to stand in faith, to trust God concerning His promises, and believe in the power of ministry partnership.

Although I continued to pray and believe for this, months went by with no word. My life was so full of ministry, I was caught by surprise when contacted and asked by Dr. Cho to join the board of Church Growth International Ministries. I still serve on that board and we still partner with his ministry.

At that time I had a very small ministry with only two or three employees. Yet, every year since becoming partners with Dr. Cho, my ministry has increased and become more and more international in scope.

As I had experienced in partnering with others, the anointing upon Dr. Cho's world outreach ministry has come upon my own. Today, I minister overseas more than I ever have, and that area of our ministry has great growth.

Principle of Ministry Partnership

Have you noticed the pattern? It took me a while to figure it out. Every time God wanted to take my ministry to a new level, He gave me the opportunity to partner with a ministry that was successfully operating in that anointing. That's what you're doing when you stand in partnership with your local church...and with a ministry God directs you to that's spreading the gospel around the world. *Each opportunity to partner with a ministry was a key to more miracles in my life and ministry.*

Once I saw the pattern, I began to study the Word to find the Biblical basis for what was happening. In the next few chapters, I'm going to briefly explain what I discovered. I was stunned by my findings and I think you will be too!

Your **Personal** *Key to Miracle Living*

If you are serious about finding *your* key to receiving more miracles in your life, you should read this book *very carefully*—word for word...line for line...page for page—from cover to cover.

Each chapter of this book is a special and unique revelation that will speak to your heart. Yet, somewhere within the pages of this book is one special chapter, or one special thought, or perhaps one special sentence that was written by the prompting of the Holy Spirit just for *you*. If you are a serious seeker of God, I guarantee that by the time you finish the last page, you will have found your key—the pathway to more miracles in your life.

• When we write down our miracle prayer needs, we clarify our thinking which enables us to pray more effectively, and that brings our prayer request a step closer to God's miracle answer. Ministry partnership has very special privileges and benefits.

• Write down the things you are believing to receive from God.

Chapter 2

⋘*Getting Back What the Devil Has Stolen*⋙

Has it ever seemed that someone "behind the scenes" was trying to sabotage your life? Just when you make a little progress, take a step forward, something happens and you slide back two steps. You're not "imagining things"; someone really is out to get you and that "someone" is your archenemy...the devil. In John 10:10, Jesus described an enemy as one whose aim is to...steal...kill...and destroy us!

Perhaps the devil has attacked your health...your marriage...your children...or your finances and the situation seems hopeless. Don't give up! I have great news. *You can take back what the devil has stolen.* You can get back kids who are living destructive lives...you can get back your marriage or other relationships...you can get back your health...you can even get back the "stuff" the devil has stolen.

David's Darkest Hour

Within the span of one day, David lost everything—his wives and everything he owned. All he had left of value was his life, and even that was in danger. This incident happened while David was living outside of Israel because King Saul was trying to kill him. As bad as things had been for David...and they had been pretty bad in the past...this was David's darkest hour.

You probably remember the course of events leading up to this point in David's life. As a shepherd boy, David was anointed to be king. Young David killed the giant, Goliath. The maidens of Israel celebrated David in song as the one who had "killed tens of thousands," while Saul, they sang, had killed only "thousands."

David was taken by Saul to the capital and given one of Saul's daughters as a wife. Eventually, Saul's jealousy of David's popularity and the anointing upon his life caused the king to try to kill David. So we join the story of David after the time he had to flee and become an outcast.

God called 600 men to join David in his exile. Most of them, like David, were society's outcasts—men with so little going for them that joining David, living in caves, and turning outlaw was preferable to their former lives. They were mostly just ordinary men, some were considered losers and failures.

Knit to Purpose...Power...and Anointing

Yet, this *same* band of *600 men* was later called David's "mighty men." What happened to them? How did they go from ordinary men and losers to lords? The Bible says that when they came to David, they were "knit" to him. That means that God connected their hearts to David's and they became his "partners in purpose"— they were partners in God's call on David's life to be the

14

king of Israel.

When you read I Samuel 23, you will discover that this band of former losers did amazing...even supernatural things. Remember that they were not famous soldiers when they came to David, just ordinary men of their time. Yet, they accomplished things far beyond their natural ability. What happened to them?

> ## An Anointing of the Word...
>
> *"One day I turned on Christian television and there was a woman* [Marilyn Hickey] *who had a knowledge of God's Word I didn't have, but needed. She didn't speak down to me but taught on a level I could understand. She helped raise me to the* [spiritual] *level I had hoped for and I'm still growing."*
>
> Beverly

When God "knit" them to David's *purpose* they received David's power—his "giant-killer" anointing. Yes, the same power, anointing, and abilities God had given David to become king came upon that group of ordinary men and made them invincible heroes. *The same thing happens when "ordinary people" partner with a ministry—they receive the supernatural anointing upon that ministry.*

From Bankrupt to Abundant

See how it works? When they committed themselves to help David achieve his God-given purpose—God supernaturally empowered them. When they came into partnership with David, they received blessings beyond their wildest hopes and dreams.

Once held in dishonor...they became the *most* honored men in Israel, once poor and bankrupt...they became the *most* wealthy, once unknown and nameless...they became the *most* famous men of their era, and many of them are even named in Scripture.

When God calls a person to partner with a ministry, He knits them, or causes a spiritual connection to be made, to that ministry. When you feel drawn toward a ministry, God's knitting needles are tugging at your heartstrings. He wants to knit you to that ministry's purpose—to connect you to the blessing, power, and anointing that He has placed on it. Don't ignore God's call and miss your blessing!

Return to Despair City

At this time, David and his men were still outlaws in Israel and working as mercenaries for the Philistine King, Achish. Achish was so pleased with David's service he gave him the city of Ziklag as a home for him and his men. *Ziklag* means "overwhelming despair."

One day, David and his men returned home to discover that their city had been looted and burned to the ground, and that their wives, sons and daughters, and all their belongings had been taken by the Amalekites.

Who do you think was "behind the scenes" prompting the Amalekites to steal from David and his men? Did God cause David's loss? NO! God is not the thief, He doesn't steal your health or your things, and He definitely doesn't want to destroy you. God wants to bless you and build you up. David had the same enemy you and I face—the devil.

This was a *turning point* in David's life. He could have...
- Given up and lost everything *including* his dream to be king.
- Ended his life by allowing his men to act out the anguish of their loss by stoning him.
- Hung his head and said, "This must be God's will for my life. He must be trying to teach me something. I'll learn so much by living with my loss. I haven't always done the right thing; I guess God is judging me. The Lord giveth and the Lord taketh away. Blessed be the name of the Lord."

David could have done the things we sometimes do or think of doing when the enemy steals from us—but he didn't.

Discouraged? Or Encouraged? It's Your Choice

The Bible says that David wiped the tears from his eyes, and according to I Samuel 30:6, "encouraged himself in the Lord." Sometimes God sends people to encourage us, other times, He expects us to do it ourselves.

What do you suppose David did to "encourage" himself? Do you think he might have recalled that God had a special purpose for his life—like He has for yours? Do you think David might have recalled when God had helped him to defeat the lion and the bear as a shepherd boy—like God has helped you through past problems?

> ## Supernatural Experience...
>
> *"Being a partner with Marilyn Hickey Ministries has been a supernatural experience for me. The Bible has opened up to me through her TV teaching and books."*   Oliver

Could David have remembered when God helped him defeat the giant—as God has defeated giants in your life? Perhaps he reminisced about the times King Saul had tried to kill him and God had made a way of escape—as He has given you a way out of your most serious situations. In your day of despair, you can do what David did...remember the times God has come to your assistance...encourage yourself in the Lord!

It's Never Too Late

When David consulted God about his dilemma, God told David to go after the things that were stolen. David and his men set out after what was rightfully theirs. When the devil has stolen from you, God's answer is never to give up. God always says the same thing, "Go after what has been stolen, it's yours by right, and I will help you to get it back."

Even if you have already given up, as David had until he encouraged himself, you can still *change your mind.* It isn't too late to dry the tears from your eyes, stand up and face your enemy, and shout, "No devil, you can't have my health, my wealth, or my children. You can't have anything of mine!" Oh, dear friend, it's never too late to get back what the devil's stolen!

Crashing Through Hell's Gates

When Jesus announced to a startled group of disciples that He was founding a Church and not a nation, He said, *"...I will build my church; and the gates of hell shall not prevail against it"* (Matthew 16:18 KJV).

As a member of Jesus' Church, you have power and authority over your enemy. When you were born again, you *partnered with Jesus* in purpose, power, and anointing. When Jesus walked the earth He demonstrated power over the devil. That's why Jesus went on to say in Matthew 16:19, *"...I will give YOU the keys of the kingdom of heaven, and whatever you bind on earth will be bound in heaven, and whatever you loose on earth will be loosed in heaven"* (NKJ).

Pakistani Calamity

I recall when the devil tried to stop my citywide Crusade in Karachi, Pakistan. After spending tens of thousands of dollars to set up the Crusade, one week before the event, we lost our permit *and* the place to hold our meeting. (I called upon our prayer warriors, staff, and this ministry's friends and partners to pray.) Two days before the meeting, when I got on the airplane to fly to Pakistan, we still didn't have a permit. When I arrived in Pakistan a day before the Crusade, we had a place to hold our meetings, but still no permit.

The morning of the Crusade—no permit. A few hours before the meeting was to begin the power of the enemy was broken and we had our meeting permit. Over 100,000 Pakistanis attended. Many of those people were Muslims and tens of thousands prayed the sinner's prayer.

You really can crash through the very gates of hell and take back what the enemy has stolen. There is a "devil defeating" anointing on this ministry that our partners can access—I've done it and so can you!

Stay With the Stuff

David and his 600 men went in hot pursuit of the enemy. When they got to the Brook Besor, a third of his men were exhausted. The Bible says that David left the weary men with their "stuff" while he and the remaining 400 men continued on the trail of the Amalekites.

David's men who stayed with the "stuff" are like the partners of a ministry. They stay and take care of the things at home, while we take the gospel to places

A Word From Sarah...

*One of the most important
things Mom and I do for our partners
is provide them with a prayer covering.
Not only do Mom and I pray for our partners
daily, our prayer warriors and the whole
ministry staff lift up their prayer
requests before God.
A concert of prayer rises to heaven on
behalf of each partner's needs.
And, the release of faith through
prayer brings miracle results
in their lives.
Don't miss out.
It really works!*

like Sudan (the former home of Osama bin Laden) or to Pakistan, bin Laden's old neighborhood. Sarah and I are called to go, but someone has to remain behind to support us financially and back us in prayer.

Surprise Attack

When David came upon the Amalekites they were having a drunken party, a victory celebration. He and his men surrounded them and had no trouble defeating them. I love what the Bible says happened next: *"So David recovered ALL that the Amalekites had carried away....NOTHING OF THEIRS WAS LACKING, either small or great, sons or daughters, spoil or anything which they had taken from them; DAVID RECOVERED ALL"* (I Samuel 30:18,19).

They took back EVERYTHING and *EVERYONE* they had lost. Not only did they get back *all* their things—they didn't lose a person...a mate, a son or daughter, or a loved one to the enemy. You don't have to lose anyone either! You don't have to give up on your unsaved husband, wife, children, or grandchildren. There is *no one* so "hard" that God can't soften their hearts. God has a way to get through to the toughest person—even that one for whom you've been praying, seemingly, forever. God got to you...didn't He? He can get to them, too!

Not only did they get back *all* they had lost, they also got the spoils the Amalekites had taken from other towns. You see, when you force the enemy to return what he has stolen, you always get it back with interest.

Your Turning Point?

When David and his 400 men returned triumphant to the 200 who had remained behind, some of his men said the spoils shouldn't be shared with those who hadn't actually been in the battle. Yet, David made a decree that would become a law throughout Israel and that law echoes a spiritual law of God's kingdom. *Those who stay behind share EQUALLY in the rewards with those who go.*

Few of our ministry partners can go with Sarah and me when we minister overseas. Yet, we who "go" and those who remain at home to support us financially and with their prayers share equally in the rewards of that outreach—the lives changed, the souls saved, and the sick that are healed. *Those who stay with the "stuff" get the "stuff."*

Could this be *your* turning point from a place of "overwhelming despair"? Could God be showing *you* how to be "knit" to an anointing that will help you reclaim what has been stolen? Could God be calling *you* to "stay with the stuff"?

Benefits for Those Who Stay Behind

I want you to see a few praise reports from our partners. These are people, like David's 200 men, who remain behind yet enjoy the benefits of the anointing upon this ministry.

A partner from Antioch, Tennessee attended one of Sarah's meetings. When Sarah said, "Tumors are being healed!" the woman's tumor disappeared.

A partner from Virginia called the Prayer Center and asked prayer for her daughter who had a lump in her breast. After prayer, she returned to the doctor for a checkup—the lump was gone!

ACTION STEP

• I want you to take out pencil and paper and make a list of everything the enemy has stolen from you.

• Don't leave anything off your list.

• Now put your hand on the list and pray after me:

"Dear Father in heaven, Your Word says that the thief must repay what has been stolen and that you will take things that were meant to harm us and turn them for our good. Lord, we ask You to cause what has been taken to be restored, and reverse the things the devil meant for our harm and turn them for our good. In Jesus' powerful name we pray. Amen."

Chapter 3

⪻*Your Key to Overflowing Blessing*⪼

Did you know that God has an overflow of blessings to meet your needs? If you're thinking, "Marilyn, you don't know how *many* needs I have." Still, God promises to meet them ALL in His Word. Right now, today, I want you to take a short vacation from the anxiety of your needs and discover how to receive God's abundant promises of an *overflowing supply* of blessing.

Does it surprise you to learn that the Apostle Paul had ministry partners? It's true. Not only did he have partners, Paul wrote them a "ministry letter." We call that letter the book of Philippians. It is no coincidence that Philippians contains a Bible verse that is a favorite for people believing for financial blessing— Philippians 4:19, *"And my God shall supply ALL your needs according to His riches in glory by Christ Jesus."*

Yet, Paul actually wrote this to the people in the church of Philippi—his *ministry partners*. The promise that God will "supply all your needs" was meant for ministry partners! I'm not saying there are no promises or blessings for people who don't partner with a ministry. Rather, I'm saying *this promise* was specifically written to partners and no one else.

How To Receive

If this is shocking news for you, stop and think for a moment. Don't many, if not all, of God's promises require you to *do* something first? Jesus said in the Sermon on the Mount, "Seek FIRST the kingdom of God...then all these things will be added unto you."

Before receiving God's greatest gift, salvation, we had to first—*believe* upon the Lord Jesus Christ. God has various "ways" of bringing blessing into our lives, and committing to ministry partnership is often an important step.

God Calls

Philippians 1:4,5 says: "*...I always pray with joy because of your PARTNERSHIP IN THE GOSPEL from the first day until now*" (NIV). Notice how Paul called the Philippians his "partners." Later in the same chapter, Paul encouraged them in their giving by reminding them that God would help them to fulfill their financial pledge. Apparently, they had promised to give a certain sum of money to Paul, taken the offering, and come up short of the amount they had promised.

Many people shy away from making pledges because they don't really understand that *the finances to complete their promise will be provided by God*. If God prompts you to partner financially with a ministry—He will provide the money for you to fulfill your promise. Remember, the Bible says that He will

A Word From Sarah…
If you have overwhelming needs in your life—God has an overflowing storehouse of blessings. Philippians 4:19 promises that God will supply the blessings you need out of "His riches"—not yours. Imagine a treasure house heaped with fabulous diamonds (some as big as your fist), rubies, emeralds, gold and silver—tons of treasure. God's storehouse is bigger and better than you can imagine. It's bigger than a supermarket stacked from floor to ceiling with blessings. In fact, God has more blessings than you have needs. Ministry partnership positions you to receive what you need to have an "abundant life" in Christ.

provide "seed to the sower." (See II Corinthians 9:10.) Sometimes, when God moves on people's hearts to become ministry partners, they respond, but fail to follow through. They quit before getting started and miss the miracles God has planned for them through ministry partnership.

Partake in the Anointing

In Philippians 1:7, Paul says that his partners "shared in his grace." The word for "grace" in Greek is *charis.* It's the root of the word *charismatic* and means "gifting of God," "enablement,"—or we might say, "anointing."

When you partner with a ministry, you "share" in its anointing. You become "hooked up" with the power and "charis" God has placed upon it. When you GIVE into an anointing…you GET a share of it.

Partners' Harvest

Toward the end of his ministry letter, Paul makes it clear that his partners can expect to receive a *financial* reward for their *financial* support. *"…You Philippians know also that in the beginning of the gospel,…no church shared with me concerning GIVING AND RECEIVING but you only"* (Philippians 4:15).

Paul's partners had learned that when they gave into a ministry, they entered into God's "economic system." You exchange *your* resources for *His* supply. God provides the "seed" to give…even out of lack. Then, when you sow the seed He's provided, you turn the "key" in the lock that opens the door to God's provision and prosperity and enables you to give—and receive—more!

Who Were Paul's Partners?

The founding of the Philippian Church (Acts 16) is filled with accounts of the supernatural. Paul's first convert and partner was the woman, Lydia. She was a prosperous businesswoman who heard the gospel, believed, and invited Paul to stay in her home.

Making a Difference...

"I became a partner with Marilyn and Sarah because I wanted to have a part in 'covering the earth with the Word.' My husband and I have an opportunity to be involved with a ministry that does things we would never be able to do on our own. My husband and I, and Marilyn and Sarah are a TEAM—together we are making a difference in lives across the world. When you become a partner, you grow, your faith grows, and your walk with God will grow."

Kathie

Lydia has a lot in common with most Christians. She didn't do *great* visible *things* for God—become a missionary to Africa or hold large healing crusades. She gave into Paul's ministry what she had—a place for him to sleep. Yet, that seemingly small and insignificant act made it possible for Paul to found the Church in Philippi.

Many Christians aren't called to hold crusades in Muslim countries or preach on every continent, as we are. They're called to *send others* to those places. Sometimes they may think their monthly partner gift of $20, $50, $100 or even more a month is just a drop in the bucket and doesn't accomplish much for the kingdom of God. That is so wrong! The overwhelming majority of partners to this ministry faithfully give a small amount every month but their *combined contributions* cause BIG results.

Slave Set Free

Another miracle in Philippi was the deliverance of the demon-possessed slave girl. You may have demonic activity going on in your life, home, or workplace. You could be under a curse or spell. Perhaps, in the past, you've had contact with demons or the occult. The slave girl was set completely free and you can be, too.

When Paul began to preach, the young slave girl with a spirit of divination (a demonic ability to allegedly foretell the future) followed Paul and Silas around and harassed them. One day, as she spoke out yet again, Paul cast the demon out of her.

You can have freedom and victory over the rule of Satan through the power of God. The anointing that comes on those who plug in to the miracle-working power of ministry partnership can break the devil's bondage and set you free.

Prison Doors Opened

The men who owned the demon-possessed slave girl were angry with Paul for ending the profitable income they expected from her fortune telling. They caused Paul and Silas to be beaten with rods and thrown in jail.

In prison, Paul and Silas had to endure the pain from their beatings along with the further torment of having their feet fastened in stocks. Yet they didn't grumble and complain. In fact, the Bible says they prayed and worshiped God while the other inmates listened. Then God caused an earthquake to strike the jail and the locked doors sprang open and their shackles and chains fell off.

Many people, even Christians, need to be set free from bondage and torment. Some may have relationships that cause torment, others have habits and addictions that seem as strong as the chains that bound Paul and Silas. Dear friend, you really can be free as you allow the miracle-working power of God that can come through ministry partnership to destroy the yoke of your bondage and bring you to a place of peace.

Family Salvation

Paul's third ministry partner was a jailer. The jailer, fearing he would be killed for allowing the inmates to escape, was ready to kill himself until Paul told him that everyone was still there. The man fell to his knees and said, "What must I do to be saved?" That same evening, as the jailer cared for his wounds, Paul spoke to the members of the jailer's family and they were ALL saved. This Philippian jailer had the miracle of a "family salvation."

When you partner with a ministry, you no longer stand alone in prayer for your unsaved family members. You have an army of prayer warriors bombarding heaven with prayers for their salvation.

Partner Miracles

I want to share with you a few praise reports that illustrate how the anointing for healings and miracles on this ministry flows down on our partners.

Not long ago, we prayed with one of our partners for her granddaughter born with Down's syndrome. She wrote back to tell us that her granddaughter is now attending "regular" school and making *A's!*

Betty, a partner from Mississippi called our Prayer Center for her pregnant daughter (whose delivery was overdue because her water wouldn't break) and for her grandson, whose birth was endangered because the umbilical cord was wrapped around his neck. After prayer, the baby was born with no complications. The doctor said he would be brain dead and deaf, but tests and reports prove that he is perfectly healthy.

> ## Finding Fertile Ground...
>
> *"This ministry is 'fertile ground.' When my wife and I give we know that we are sowing into good ground. Marilyn and Sarah are bringing salvation to people around the world in the many countries in which they minister. We can support this ministry wholeheartedly knowing that our monthly support is going into fertile ground."*
> Jerry

Get "Plugged In" for Your Miracle

The anointing and blessings upon Paul came down on the people who became his partners. His anointing overflowed into their lives and caused their personal situations to be "turned around." Your decision to become a partner could turn your problems around, too.

Isn't it time for the miracle-working power of ministry partnership to begin operating in your life? Your partnership will cause Philippians 4:19—the ministry partners' promise—to operate in your life.

ACTION STEP

• Jesus instructed us to take authority over our problems by speaking to them. In Mark 11:23, He said, *"...whoever SAYS TO THIS MOUNTAIN, 'Be removed and be cast into the sea,' and does not doubt in his heart, but believes that those things he says will come to pass, he will have whatever he says."*

• So dear friend, lift up your hands to God and speak Philippians 4:19 ALOUD over your needs. Say, *"...My God will meet all* [my] *needs according to his glorious riches in Christ Jesus"* (Philippians 4:19,20 NIV).

• Repeat this verse until it echoes in your mind...until it shouts down the voice of your anxieties and fears.

Chapter 4

⟨⟩ Empowered To Do the Supernatural ⟨⟩

D ear Reader,
  I love watching God "work"! Over the years, I have seen His hand in this ministry...in our church...and in our family. What God is doing in the lives of my children and grandchildren—it is pure "dynamite"!

  Now, my daughter Sarah and I are working to "cover the earth with the Word"...together. Imagine! God called her into this ministry, and the same anointing for healings and miracles is now powerfully present in her life. I am convinced that the greatest times are ahead and that Sarah will see greater miracles and more salvations than I can imagine!

  Growing up as a "p.k." (preachers' kid) and, now, being in the ministry herself, Sarah has witnessed and experienced first-hand the blessings of ministry partnership countless times. I know that as you read what Sarah is about to share from her heart, new doorways of blessing will open up in your life!

  Marilyn Hickey

Mom and I have ministered in so many countries and no two nations—or even people groups—are alike. The uniqueness is uncanny! Still, there is *one thing* every person on this planet desires—to lead a full …rich…rewarding…productive…powerful life. Regardless of where you are or where you've been *you want that, too*!

That is the message I am so strongly impressed to share with you. You'll want to catch every bit of it! So stick with me, because in these next few pages, we'll learn that "the good life" IS attainable…and we'll discover an important key—a "God key"—to getting there.

The Mandate To "Dream Big"

The desire for God's best is built into the heart of every human being. We want good things to happen to us— loving relationships…peace in our hearts…significance… purpose…the best of health…abundant provision.

The Word Is Going Forth...

"I believe in what [Marilyn's] doing….The Word is going forth and partners are helping her get the Word out, to the glory of God. We love the Lord with all of our hearts and she's doing what we believe ought to be done…going where angels fear to tread…she is just without fear….We join her in doing this and we've become courageous and strong….We're just glad to be part of it." Nona

Wanting these things is not shallow or greedy. These dreams are based in the very plan of God. We long for "good-ness" to surround us. So did David. In Psalms 27:13, he eagerly looked to *"...see the goodness of the LORD in the land of the living"* (NIV).

God fashioned us exactly that way. We're His children, designed to think as He does. The Bible says we were created in His image and likeness. So, we naturally reach upward. Our innate tendency—*whether we admit it or even realize it*—is to "think big," as though *nothing were impossible*.

That's right where God wants us, because *everything IS possible...with Him.* Depending upon your personal experience, a statement like that will do one of two things: bless your socks off, or make your head spin. Either way— it's gospel truth. Luke 1:37 says it point blank: *"...Nothing is impossible with God"* (NIV).

There's the Promise...NOW... Where's the Power?

Notice, the Bible says nothing is impossible *with God*. Left on our own, lots of things are impossible. We can drive ourselves so hard trying to "make something happen"—as though we were the "power source"— and then wonder why things don't turn out the way we planned.

The promises of God are rock solid—but we need to approach them God's way. The *secret is in the source* and the *key is empowerment*. I'm not talking about electric power or solar power or even nuclear power. The power we need is divine...supernatural... breakthrough-producing power...a power that often requires us to *join with others* to achieve God's best together.

Our *source* is God. He *empowers* us by teaching us the way His system works. He doesn't hide the keys to His kind of success—He freely reveals them to us, because *He desires our prosperity as much as we do!* Once we take the keys from His hand, He pours out the bounty of His provision.

The power we desire—the power we *need*—to live the "all-things-are-possible" life comes from God!

Cover the Earth? How?

When God called my mom to "cover the earth with the Word," she was a busy pastor's wife with two children. At the time, she couldn't imagine accomplishing such a task. She was certain that a homemaker from Denver lacked the qualifications needed to do something so "big."

So, Mom did what she knew to do—she stuck close to God and walked through the doors He opened for her. She realized the vision was God's and it would be *His* power that would get the job done.

Little by little, the pieces began to fall into place.

People volunteered to help answer ministry mail. (The "office" was our kitchen table.) Invitations to minister began to come in. Day by day, God showed Mom more and more of the picture.

People began to partner with Mom. As the ministry grew, Mom saw how God was making a way for her to obey Him. Suddenly, "covering the earth with the Word" was an attainable goal. Today, the ministry employs more than three hundred people and Mom and I minister all over the world.

God gets all the glory, because only He can empower an *ordinary person* to do extraordinary things.

Did You Say "Preach... to EVERY Creature"?

Peter, Matthew, John, and the other disciples were ordinary men, too. Jesus handpicked His team, but He didn't select powerful politicians, military heroes, or brilliant philosophers to change the world. Jesus chose fishermen, tax collectors, manual laborers—and *transformed* them into world-changers.

Jesus sent His team to *"...go into all the world and preach the gospel to every creature"* (Mark 16:15). From a human perspective, He had asked them to do what was clearly impossible, but as world history and the Word of God confirm, they turned the world upside down!

It wasn't the disciples' personal credentials that

enabled them to be effective—it was the power and anointing that resulted from their vital connection ...their *partnership*...with Jesus that *empowered* them to revolutionize the world.

When Jesus commissioned them, He was putting His name on the line, not theirs. All He asked of them was to partner *with Him*. This vital partnership is still impacting the world today!

Reach for the Power Switch

God designed us for *maximum* impact *living*, too. PLEASE HEAR THIS and let it seep into the depths of your soul: *God didn't create you to live a hum-drum life of just getting by and wishing for a better tomorrow. He never meant for you to live confined within the boundaries of your natural abilities and personal resources.*

No way! God has a place of no-holds-barred, supernatural, bondage-breaking mega life with your name on it! If you will grasp the same principles that "switched the power on" for the disciples, you will rise above your disappointments and defeats and reach beyond your limitations to a new level of power, significance, and prosperity.

That "power switch" is partnership. Nobody can do anything truly great all by themselves. The disciples became involved in something bigger than any one man or woman. They became part of a vision that superseded their own thinking. They partook of the

Lives Are Changed...

"[Partnership] *has changed our lives. I mean it sincerely—it has changed our lives. We have developed so much in our walk with the Lord....It is directly connected, of course, with our church, but also with being a part of Marilyn's ministry."*

Coleman

anointing that so saturated them it overwhelmed the strongholds of their personal limitations. They joined a "supernatural team"—and stepped up to a level none of them had dared to imagine.

The disciples went beyond themselves...beyond their limited experience...beyond the realm of impossibility. They surged past where they'd been and the opinions of others. They began to taste of the supernatural—a life that had always seemed to be beyond their reach.

They found the "power switch" in partnership. So can *you*!

Power Flows From the Head

Power and authority flow in much the same way in the kingdom of God as in the secular world. Military personnel and corporate employees understand that whatever is "going on at the top" affects everyone down the line.

In the spiritual realm, we say the anointing that is

on the head flows down to the body. God instructed Moses on how to consecrate his brother Aaron as High Priest. He said, *"And you shall take the anointing oil, pour it on his head, and anoint him"* (Exodus 29:7). As Aaron was *anointed* with oil, God gave him the ability to act in a supernatural capacity.

Imagine how the oil poured on Aaron's head dripped down all over him. It touched his face…his beard…his body, even though Moses specifically poured the oil on Aaron's head as God had commanded. Psalms 133:2 shows us a picture of the anointing oil flowing from the head down: *"It is like the precious oil upon the head, running down on the beard, the beard of Aaron, running down on the edge of his garments."*

Aaron was High Priest of Israel consecrated for service while en route to the Promised Land. Jesus is now our High Priest for all eternity. He is the Head of the Body (which is the Church). We are Christ's body. Just as the oil flowed from Aaron's head to his body, so the anointing flows from Jesus to His Body of believers.

Transference—The "Power Pipeline"

My grandmother, my mom and dad, and my husband and I have partnered with a number of ministries over the years, among them Oral Roberts, T.L. Osborne, and Dr. David Yonggi Cho. In each case, the anointing on the head of the ministry has flowed down—or been *transferred*—to our lives and ministries. The anointings for healing, miracles, and nations have manifested in a significant way each time we have partnered with others.

This transference of anointing is not accidental or coincidental. It is Biblical—an important way in which God chooses to build His kingdom. In fact, examples of the transference of anointing are found throughout the Old and New Testaments.

One "method" of transference is the laying on of hands. (See Numbers 8:10-14; Acts 28:8,9; Acts 9:17,18; I Timothy 4:14.) Jesus Himself spoke of laying on of hands in the Great Commission: *"...They will lay hands on the sick, and they will recover"* (Mark 16:18). This is a transference of the healing anointing.

Transference of anointing is not restricted to the laying on of hands, however. In his letter to the Philippians, Paul spoke specifically to his partners regarding the transference of the blessings upon his ministry: *"We have shared together the blessings of God, both when I was in prison and when I was out, defending the truth and telling others about Christ"* (TLB). Paul's partners shared his blessing because they were "on his team."

We see that time and again in our ministry. Partners write us letters all the time...people like Debra, who shared how God had brought her additional work to meet her needs—and made it possible for her son to change his work schedule so he could attend Sunday services. Or Bernice, who now has a new, higher-paying job as a corporate developer. These women have seen the anointing for "breakthrough" power that marks this ministry come upon their own lives.

Giving AND *Receiving*

Paul's partners experienced the same kind of transference. Think of it this way—whatever Paul did, his partners *had a part* in doing. Whatever fruit resulted from his ministry was *their fruit*, too! His reward was *their reward*. The anointing on his life was on their lives...simply because they entered into partnership with Him.

Partnership is NOT a one-way street. There's more to it than writing out a check each month. In fact, although financial support meets very real needs, partnership runs deeper than that. When you share your finances with a ministry, you are saying, "I'm making a supernatural connection with you. My destiny is now intertwined with yours. Here's a *piece*

Thankful for Partnership...

"Praise God! I thank Marilyn Hickey....I thank God for Sarah and the work they're doing around the world....They have changed our lives. This is the sixth [ministry] *trip I have been on* [with this ministry]. *Many souls are saved and many miracles* ....[You should] *come and see the awesome mighty ...miracle-working God do His thing!"*

Gwen

of my life as a symbol of my commitment to the vision God has given you."

Partners are partakers! God honors your commitment. If He calls you to partner with a ministry, He wants you to *partake* of its anointing. Whatever you sow into, becomes a part of your life.

In turn, our partners become a part of our family and their testimonies become a part of our lives. It's so encouraging to see our partners reap the benefits of ministry partnership. Mom tells the story of a man named Dave. Some years ago, he got healed of colon cancer at one of Mom's encounters—*and* he had $83,000 of credit card debt miraculously cancelled! The anointing on this ministry came to rest upon Dave and eliminated his cancer and cancelled his debt—what a testimony!

More recently, during one of our Women's Mentoring Clinics, one of the ladies stood up to pray for people with problems in their mouths. Twenty or 25 women stood up for prayer, including a lady who was missing two teeth. She was believing for her teeth to be restored—and that's exactly what happened. God gave her two new teeth! Miraculous! The anointing for healings and miracles that is on this ministry flowed through the women who prayed—and God created two new teeth for a woman who needed them!

One of our partners called for prayer because she had a lump in her breast. After prayer, the lump was gone! Her doctor couldn't find it. A mammogram proved the miracle clearly—NO LUMP. When you get involved with God and the anointing, all things are possible!

People who partner with this ministry also tell us how their hunger for the Word increases. That is another example of the transference of a fundamental anointing that is on this ministry. Mom and I can't get enough of God's Word. We are called to COVER THE EARTH with it! You can't cover the earth with the Word if you're not full of the Word yourself, so God has anointed us with a deep desire to devour His Word.

Our partners share with us in all of the blessings of this ministry. Gifts of healings, miracles, anointed teaching, and a heart for nations are just some of the things shared by our ministry partners.

All of this is by God's design. He knows it takes a team to "cover the earth with His Word" so, through partnership, He handpicks the team members we need—people who need the anointing that is on this ministry. It's a perfect plan!

Just as He has blessed us through the ministries with which we have partnered, He is blessing *our partners* with the "overflow" of the anointing that rests on us. At the same time, He is providing—through our partners' prayers and giving—what it takes to continue to reach people and nations with the life-changing gospel of Jesus Christ.

Like my mom, I just *love* watching God "work"—to

see firsthand the thrilling things He's doing *through* our ministry partners' faithfulness and *in* their lives. We've got a supernatural, life-giving connection that takes all of us to the level of the extraordinary...together —to do...to be...and to have all that God has promised us.

That's the *power of partnership* at work. Let that power work FOR YOU!

• Close your eyes and visualize this future event: Someone in heaven will come up to you and say, "Thank you for changing my eternal destiny!"

• You'll reply, "I've never even *met* you."

• But—through your partnership with a ministry involved in world missions—their destiny was changed. And because you had a share in the miracle, the reward is yours, too.

Chapter 5

⟨⟩Faith Alliance–Join the War⟨⟩
Against Terror

I get passionate about the terrorism that is going on around the world. Terrorism is a hideous thing...but as bad as world terrorism is—the devil's terrorist attack on Christians is even worse. Yet, if you and I get into a "faith alliance," we can confidently battle the devil's terrorist attack upon your life...absolutely break the back of darkness...and have total victory.

Advanced Warning

When George W. Bush was finally inaugurated President, I was in London. I remember sitting in my hotel room watching the ceremony on CNN. As I watched, God spoke to my heart in a powerful way. He told me that our President faced great danger and needed to be surrounded with a wall of prayer.

God didn't tell me the specifics...He didn't allude to the coming tragedy of September 11th. Yet, God did give me an overwhelming sense of urgency. When I returned to the U.S., I shared what God had told me with key people in my ministry and we made plans to enlist the partners and friends of this ministry into a *faith alliance* to surround President Bush with daily prayer. We invited more than 100,000 people to join this prayer effort and on September 11—we discovered why God had called us to prayer.

President Bush was clearly one of the targets of the terrorist attack. I believe the President and his family were spared because of the prayers of our *faith alliance* and others across the country. Through prayer, we stood between the President and the devil's murderous plans. Because we had joined together in a *faith alliance* of prayer what could have happened...didn't. As bad as this tragedy was—it would have been much worse without our combined prayers.

THINK ABOUT THIS: *What if your life*—like President Bush's—*was covered by a faith alliance that could defend you against terrorist attacks of the devil and bring you to complete victory?*

Such a Time...

Just as God prepared a *faith alliance* of protection and wisdom to pray for President Bush before he needed it, God prepared a way of escape from genocide for His people long ago when they were captives in Persia.

Even before the enemy hatched his conspiracy to kill all the Jews, God had placed Esther in the position of Queen of the Persian Empire to thwart the plan. With a death threat hanging over their heads, the Jewish people came together in a *faith alliance* of prayer and fasting to back Esther's daring intercession for their lives before the king. The result was that the

Jewish people were saved from their enemy. God put a halt to one of the devil's darkest and most dangerous terrorist attacks.

I feel in my spirit that some who are reading these words are in a similar dark and dangerous place. The chief terrorist, Satan, has struck somewhere in your life. He wants to destroy you...or someone or something precious to you. This message and the principles of ministry partnership could be God's provision for your deliverance.

My Gift Goes Around the World...

"I believe in Marilyn Hickey Ministries and its outreach to the world. I know that my partner gift helps Marilyn and Sarah to go around the world to preach the gospel."
Debra

Perhaps your children or a loved one are running headlong down the road to destruction ...maybe your finances have you teetering on the brink of disaster...or possibly you've been attacked directly—you have a disease or illness that threatens your very life. *Whatever it is*, you know you need help. A *faith alliance* through ministry partnership can stop the terror—once and for all—and prevent the success of the enemy's terrorist attack on you or someone you love.

51

Pyramid of Power

The first thing I want to tell you is—you are mightier than you *think* or *feel*. In the natural world, one person alone could never be equal in strength and power to four or five opponents. Yet, in the kingdom of God things are *very* different. According to Deuteronomy 32:30, *"...one* [can] *chase a thousand...."* As a born-again Christian, you have an anointing on your life that makes you superior in the spirit realm to a thousand terrorists who would come against you.

One plus one equals two, right? Wrong! God uses a *higher* form of math. When God adds one plus one, He gets 10,000. That's right! When you join forces with another believer, God says in Deuteronomy 32:30, *"...two put ten thousand to flight...."* Imagine what can be done when tens of thousands of Christians join together in an alliance against the enemy!

Dear friend, when you come into partnership with a ministry, you and that ministry are unstoppable. Do you see? Together, we really can put the devil to flight...in your life...our nation...and the entire world. "If God is for us, who *can* stand against us?" (See Romans 8:31.)

Victims of the Terror

Many people, for one reason or another, consider themselves victims. Our world would have us believe that each of us is in some way a victim—the victim of a dysfunctional family, victim of an uncaring mate, victim of "big" business or government, victim of prejudice, victim of a poor education. The list goes on and on. It is easy for Christians who are terrorized by Satan to feel like they are victims, too.

The fact is, no one had a perfect upbringing, everyone has had negative experiences in life, and the devil *does* attack Christians. Some people have been so abused, terrorized, and harassed by him they have given up all hope for a better tomorrow. Everything is bad and getting worse—going from gloom to doom. Do you ever feel that way?

Yet, in the face of all your problems...the Bible declares that you *are not* a victim...rather, you *are* a victor. Romans 8:35,37 says, *"Who shall separate us from the love of Christ? Shall tribulation, or distress, or persecution, or famine, or nakedness, or peril, or sword?...Yet in all these things WE ARE MORE THAN CONQUERORS through Him who loved us."*

If you've fallen into a pit of defeat...and you've tried to climb out on your own, but you just can't make it. You need someone to toss you a rope and pull you out. Connecting with a faith-based ministry—joining a *faith alliance*—can extend to you a *life*line and be your means of rescue and release.

Turn the Table on the Terrorist

You don't have to take it anymore! You can remove the bull's eye from your back and refuse to be a target for

Confidence in Marilyn's Integrity...

"When I listen to Marilyn, I know that she is a real woman of God and I have confidence that my financial support will go for what God intended. I want to be a part of a ministry like that and I know that I'll be blessed for it."

Stacia

the devil's terror! In fact, isn't it about time for you to turn the tables on the devil and terrorize *him?* Jesus empowered you to put the devil where he belongs— under your feet! He said, *"Behold, I give you the authority to trample on serpents and scorpions, and OVER ALL THE POWER OF THE ENEMY, and nothing shall by any means hurt you"* (Luke 10:18).

The devil fears the day that you understand how *mighty* you are in Christ. He quakes at the thought of the damage you could do to his plans if you ever *really believed* and started using the authority Jesus has given you. The enemy's strategy to neutralize and eliminate you as a threat is to keep you facedown in the mud...a "victim" in your own mind.

You may be thinking, "Marilyn, if I have 'authority' why are things so terrible in my life?" Oh, friend, *having* authority isn't enough...you have to *use* it or you lose it. If you have a gun when a lion attacks, but never draw and fire it, he will eat you just as if you had *no* weapon at all.

This ministry of the Word and faith can arm and equip you to face the *terrorist of your life*. In addition, we would count it an honor to stand alongside you spiritually to face down and utterly defeat the devil and all his personal acts of terrorism in your life.

Testimonies of Devil Defeaters

I want to relate a few testimonies from some of our partners who, as a part of our *faith alliance*, have chased the devil out of their lives.

One partner who was "harassed" by a car accident wrote us to say she had just received a big insurance settlement. *The devil lost in the end!*

Another partner wrote to tell us that her husband who had left her, came home last month. God had spoken to his heart and told him to return to his wife and live for Him just as he had when first married. *The devil can't destroy your marriage!*

Linda, a partner in Texas wrote to say that she planted a seed-faith gift into this ministry and God provided the means for her whole family to fly to California to visit her parents. While in California, she was able to pray with her 85-year-old grandmother to receive salvation. *The devil is defeated in your family!*

Seen With Their Own Eyes...

"There are so many benefits to being a partner with a dynamic ministry that has both integrity and a love for lost souls. Because we are partners with Marilyn and Sarah, we have a part in everything this ministry does. Plus, we have a part in their anointing. When we can, we love to travel overseas and minister, literally, side-by-side with Marilyn. We've seen with our own eyes thousands of lives changed, souls won, people healed and we have even played a part in some of those outreaches. I suppose we could live without being partners with Marilyn and Sarah but we wouldn't miss out on this blessing for anything."

Mary

A partner wrote to tell me that while she was on surgical leave her friend at work told her that their boss was plotting to get rid of her. God caused her to heal supernaturally fast from the surgery and she is back on the job and has "great favor" with her boss. *The devil can't steal your job!*

A partner writes to say that her runaway son was living a horrible life on the streets and they had lost all contact with him. We stood with her in prayer and God brought Christians into her son's life. They provide him a home. His life has turned around. Now, he has a regular job and has given his heart to Jesus. Can you imagine that mother's joy when she learned that her son is off the streets and in the arms of Jesus? *The devil can't have your children either.*

The friends who join with Sarah and me in ministry partnership become a part of our family. We place a "prayer covering" over our partners every day and have a prayer center staffed with prayer warriors for them to call with their special prayer needs. When our partners are suffering, we stand with them in prayer and fight the good fight of faith until they win over the devil.

A Devil-Defeating Ministry

Each time we go to Pakistan, the devil tries to undermine or sabotage our efforts. In spite of his plot and ploys, we hold citywide crusades that hundreds of thousands attend and nationwide Ministry Training Schools for thousands of pastors and Christian leaders. Without fail, we see tens of thousands of Pakistanis (mostly Muslims) pray the sinner's prayer. None of that would be possible if we hadn't learned how to overcome the evil one. And, you can do it, too!

Regardless of how bad things are today, God has promised you an exciting, fulfilling, and *overcoming life*. Yet, to get from where you are to the new place of victory God has for you...you will have to find victory over the terrorist of your life. Partnering with the anointing upon a devil-defeating ministry allows *YOU* to walk away the winner!

ACTION STEP

• We want to form a *faith alliance* with you that will cause you to walk away a winner over the terrorism of the devil. What do you need? What can we stand with you for?

• First, mark the boxes below with your prayer needs.

❏ Unsaved or backslidden family members or friends
❏ Finances for a new house or new car
❏ Healing for yourself or a loved one
❏ Wisdom for a career move
❏ A new job or promotion
❏ Debts that need to be demolished
❏ Other _____

• Second, call our Prayer Center and ask one of the prayer warriors to agree with you in prayer for your need.

CALL RIGHT NOW!

For prayer, call TOLL-FREE, weekdays, 6:30 a.m. to 4:30 p.m. [MT] at 1-877-661-1249 (U.S only) or go to www.mhmin.org to send us your prayer request.

Chapter 6

⪻How To See Your Dreams Come True⪼

Do you have the seed of a dream growing inside you? Are you carrying a deep-down longing in your heart for some "specific" things to transpire in your life? Besides your salvation, the most important thing you possess is your dreams.

Has it always been your "dream" to write a book, go to school, travel to certain lands, see your loved ones get saved, get involved in missions, achieve financial freedom, own a house or a better car, or to use your talents in a more meaningful way?

Dreams are desires that God plants like seeds in our hearts. *God has given me a passion to see your dreams come to pass.* Years ago, the Holy Spirit spoke to me and showed me how to make dreams come true…and I want to share with you what He revealed to me.

What Are Dreams—Really?

Dreams are the language of the Holy Spirit. When you read through the Bible from Genesis to Revelation, you discover that God has used dreams to communicate with people.

Almost 100 verses of Scripture speak about dreams.

God has used dreams to communicate with both saved and unsaved people, with emperors of vast kingdoms and ordinary people.

Dreams don't always come at night while you sleep. Dreams sometimes are simply desires within us. Dreams or desires from God are very important because they provide us direction in life. Proverbs 29:18 says, *"Where there is no vision, the people perish...."* Without a dream, we have no direction in life.

Dreams of Greatness

When the Holy Spirit began to speak to me about dreams, He directed my attention to perhaps the best-known dreamer in the Bible, Joseph.

You probably remember this Bible story. Joseph was the next-to-youngest son of Jacob, whom God had renamed *Israel*. At the age of 17, Joseph had two dreams. In one dream, sheaves of grain representing Joseph's brothers bowed down to Joseph's sheaf. When Joseph told his dream to his brothers they were angry.

To make matters worse, Joseph had a second dream. In this dream, he saw the sun, moon, and eleven stars bow to him. This dream even upset his father. Jacob said, "Now your mother and I, as well as your brothers, will bow down to you?"

Had one of your younger brothers or sisters had such dreams, you probably would have had the same reaction as Joseph's brothers. They considered his dreams to be egotistical teenage fantasies and, added to the fact their father favored Joseph, it caused them to hate him.

Dreamer's Dilemma

Joseph was his father's favorite. The Bible says that Joseph was a "child of Jacob's old age." In addition, Jacob made Joseph the administrator of all his property and gave him a "coat of many colors" to attest to his high position.

FIRST DREAM PRINCIPLE:
Don't Give Up Your Dream

Joseph came under great pressure from his family to give up his dreams and so will you. The criticism of those closest to us can be a deadly assault upon our dreams. You may be misunderstood and your family may think you're crazy, too.

Undoubtedly, Joseph wanted the love and approval of his brothers and the respect of his father. Yet, Joseph knew that his dreams were from God and he refused to give them up to gain the approval of his loved ones.

You must develop the determination of Joseph concerning your dreams. Don't allow any-*one* or any-*thing* to steal them. The truth is, no one can *steal* your dreams, they can only persuade you to give them up. No matter what—don't give up your dreams.

Life Is the Pits

Joseph suffered for his dreams. You probably remember the next part of the story, when Joseph went to visit his brothers in the fields. They grabbed him, took his coat, threw him in a pit, and then sold him into slavery. To cover up their deed, they tore the many-colored coat and dabbed it in blood. Then they told their bereaved father that a wild animal must have eaten his beloved Joseph. Dreams have a price—often, the bigger the dream, the higher the price.

Do you dream of getting a higher education? You will have to study. Dream of finding the right mate? You may have to do things to make yourself more attractive as a husband or wife. Desire to be used by God? You will have to prepare and be willing to start small. Dreams carry a cost—a cost in time, effort, and determination.

Dream Maker...Heartbreaker

Often your dreams will have to undergo a "death process." You may come to the end of yourself and discover that your passion, efforts, gifts, and abilities are not enough to make your dreams come true. Although you have held fast to your dreams, this is the time to hand your dreams back to God—the One Who gave them to you in the first place.

Though it may break your heart, you must be resigned to give them up to God. You must be willing to say, "I want *Your will* more than I want this dream.

So I put my dreams into your hands to fulfill or forbid. I will love and serve You no matter what."

When you put your faith in the Dream Maker—God, He will bring a resurrection to your dreams and *supernaturally* bring them to pass. You see, if it's a God-given dream—God will be the One to fulfill it.

Seen the Love Firsthand...

"I love Marilyn's ministry and what she does. Marilyn is a down to earth person committed to what God is doing through her. She has a love for God's people and the lost. I've been with her on ministry trips and seen firsthand the hunger she has for the lost all over the world."

Brenda

Practice Means Promotion

Young Joseph was taken by the slave trader to Egypt and sold to the wealthy Egyptian, Potiphar. Joseph worked hard, using his gift of administration, and God gave him favor. Soon, Potiphar noticed Joseph's work ethic and abilities and promoted him, putting him in charge of his entire estate.

SECOND DREAM PRINCIPLE:
Practice Your Dream

I've known people who say they're called to be great healing evangelists. Yet, when asked if they have been to Bible school, if they're active in their church, or if they pray for the sick, they say, "No." When asked what they *are* doing, they say, "I'm waiting for God to set up my first citywide crusade." God expects you to prepare and practice for your dream.

What Joseph did was *uncommon* for a person in his position. It would have been more *common* for Joseph to be homesick, disillusioned, lost, and bitter over his fate. Why didn't Joseph fall apart? He was holding on to the only thing left to him, his dreams. Joseph wasn't lost because his dreams gave him direction in life. Joseph did the only positive thing he could, he practiced and prepared for the realization of his dream.

Seduction of a Dream

You probably know what happened to Joseph next. Potiphar's wife tried to seduce him. When Joseph tried to escape her advances, she grabbed his coat and presented it as proof of attempted rape. (Did you notice that Joseph lost another coat? The devil can steal your coat, but he can't steal your dreams.)

You, too, will have to resist a seduction that would steal your dream by stealing your heart and integrity. The devil doesn't want you to realize your dreams and he will tempt you with substitute "desires." Like Joseph, you must single-mindedly focus on your dreams...refuse the enemy's enticing substitutes...and keep preparing and practicing.

Dreams and Dungeons

Who would think there was something worse than slavery? It must have seemed to Joseph that his life had reached a new low when he was incarcerated in Pharaoh's prison. Once again, Joseph refused to be angry or bitter. The Bible says that God showed Joseph mercy by giving him favor with the prison administrator.

God's mercy didn't take Joseph out of the dungeon...it just made the dungeon more bearable. Plus, it gave Joseph more opportunity for—you may have guessed it—practice and preparation. Joseph became the prisoner administrator of the dungeon. What better place could there be for a farm boy from Canaan to learn the inner workings of administration for the most advanced empire of its time?

Eventually, Pharaoh sent his chief butler and chief baker to prison and they came into Joseph's care. One night, both men had dreams. When Joseph checked on his charges the next morning, they were sad because there was no one to interpret their dreams. Then Joseph did a remarkable thing. In spite of the fact it didn't look as though *his own dreams* would come to pass, he interpreted *their dreams*.

THIRD DREAM PRINCIPLE:
Sow Into the Dreams of Others

I learned this principle at a time when I was *ready* to

realize my dream of having a radio and TV ministry. In fact, I was beyond "ready." Like Joseph, I was eager to get out of the box that I felt limited my ministry, and get on with the dreams God had given me. During that time, God taught me how to make dreams come true.

I resolutely sought the Lord for the way to make the big step into television. His answer surprised me. Instead of a clever strategy, God told me, "Marilyn, until you *sow into the dreams of others* you will never have your dreams fulfilled." It was the worst time financially for me to give to another ministry. Yet, I discovered that the *worst time* for us is the *best time* for God, because it is *faith time*. It requires trust in Him. I'm here to tell you it works! However, you must understand, it doesn't work instantly.

Microwave Dreams

Joseph asked the chief butler to remember him when he returned to his position in Pharaoh's court. Yet, the butler forgot about Joseph. It was two full years before Joseph would see the door to his dungeon open and his dreams begin to be fulfilled.

This is the most critical part of this teaching, so pay special attention.

Joseph was now 30 years old. It had been 13 long and difficult years since he had received his dreams. After so long a time, Joseph could have doubted his dreams—doubted they were of God. He could easily have finally accepted the judgment of his family that his dreams were merely egotistical fantasies. It would have been easy, and some would say "natural," for Joseph to let go of his dreams.

We want our dreams to come to pass in 13 minutes...13 days...13 months...or 13 seconds. However, there is a *process* to go through before your dreams *can* come true...and there are *principles* you have to follow.

Some of you reading these words have given up your dreams—dreams for a better life, a better job, a ministry, or the salvation of a loved one. *Time cannot steal your dreams unless you let them go.* If you have dropped your dreams, it isn't too late to pick them up again.

If you have a witness in your heart—right now—that God wants you to take back your dreams—repent for losing faith in Him *and* your dreams. Dust off your dreams...strap them on...get back into the process...and use the dream

Reaching the World...

"I would tell anyone that's thinking about becoming a partner this is definitely good ground to sow in...This ministry is reaching the world and providing training [for others in] *how to do it."*
Vanessa

principles. The time will come when, like Joseph, there will be a knock on *your* door and the opportunity will arrive for *your* dreams to come true.

Your Day Will *Come*

As you may recall, Pharaoh had two powerful dreams that his court magicians couldn't interpret, and he mentioned them to his butler. The butler finally remembered Joseph and told Pharaoh about Joseph's ability to interpret dreams. Pharaoh summoned Joseph to appear before him. Joseph shaved, cleaned himself up, and stood before the most powerful man in the world. He had one more opportunity to sow into the dreams of another.

Joseph told Pharaoh that his dreams meant that Egypt would have seven years of great abundance followed by seven years of great famine. He also suggested that Pharaoh would need a wise man to organize the gathering, storing, and distributing of the food. When Pharaoh chose Joseph to be that man— second only to himself in power and authority throughout the land—Joseph's dream finally came true!

Had Joseph not practiced on his father's holdings, on Potiphar's estate, and in the prison, he would never have been able to supervise the wealth of an entire nation. *All his practice and preparation had a purpose.* They weren't merely chores that God didn't care about but allowed into Joseph's life, they were planned by

God to prepare Joseph for the fulfillment of his dream.

The same could be true for you, dear friend. The very thing you are asking God to deliver you from may actually be His preparation for the fulfillment of your dreams. If you find yourself in a dungeon-like situation far beneath the level of your dream—don't despair— God knows you're there. You're in the process of preparation for *your dreams* to be fulfilled.

Remember the two coats Joseph lost?...the "coat of many colors" and the coat at Potiphar's house? Now was time for Joseph to recover what the enemy had stolen. Pharaoh gave him the finest of coats, placed his ring of authority upon Joseph's finger, and gave him the second finest chariot in the land. The time will come when the devil will have to give back what he has stolen, and when he does, it will be better than what was taken.

FOURTH DREAM PRINCIPLE:
Forgive Those Who Have Wronged You

If you refuse to let go of your dream...practice your dream...and sow into the dreams of others, one day, you will be living your dream. You, like Joseph, will have the opportunity to take vengeance upon those who have wronged you, tried to destroy your dream, and perhaps physically or mentally abused you. It may be the hardest thing you'll ever have to do, but there is no place in your dreams for vengeance. You must forgive or your dream will become your nightmare.

When Joseph's brothers came to him in Egypt to buy food during the famine, he forgave them of all the harm they had done him. Joseph recognized God's hand in everything that had happened to him. He said to his brothers, "You meant it for evil, but God used it for good."

Dream Checkup

If you follow these four dream principles, I guarantee your dreams will be fulfilled.

Are you...
• Holding on to your dream?
• In the process—practicing and preparing?
• Sowing into the dreams of others?
• Willing to forgive?
Where are you on the path to realizing your dreams?

Dream the Impossible Dream

Many years ago now, God gave me a dream to "cover the earth with His Word." Can you imagine that God called me, a former schoolteacher, pastor's wife, and mother to do that? That's a vast dream far beyond the power and abilities of any one person. Yet, today, we are in the process of doing just that.

Over the years, God has brought me new opportunities and people to join forces with my dream. I now have my daughter, Sarah, her husband, Reece, and a dedicated staff of people who share this dream—people who are sowing their lives, talents, and abilities into that dream. I want to remind you of the third dream principle God spoke to my heart when my dreams were just getting off the ground: "Until you sow into the dreams of others you will never have your dreams fulfilled."

Sowing Into Another's Dream

I could give you thousands of instances, but let me tell you about one of my ministry partners, Jonye, who recently wrote to tell me about sowing into the dream of this ministry. She tells the story of her husband's new truck that was wrecked because of the actions of a hit-and-run driver. Although her husband skidded across three lanes of a busy expressway, he was not injured, but when the truck plowed into a concrete wall, it was severely damaged. They were thankful that his life had been spared, but disappointed because of the damage to their new truck. The driver who caused the accident had sped away from the scene.

The police told them it was unlikely that they could do anything concerning the driver who had caused the accident. Jonye and her husband filed their insurance claim, paid the $500 deductible, and began to believe that God would somehow supernaturally repay the money.

Not long afterward, they received a ministry letter from me. I asked them to consider sowing a seed into this ministry's dream while believing to see their own dream come true—they responded. Although they were hurting financially because of the accident and could have used the money to pay bills, they sowed a $50 offering. Two weeks later, their dream came true when their insurance company sent back their $500 deductible.

Is the Holy Spirit speaking to you to sow into the dreams of this ministry by becoming a ministry partner...so you can see your own dreams fulfilled? Then SOW as the Holy Spirit leads you, follow the dream principles, and YOU WILL REAP the harvest of YOUR DREAMS. It worked for me...it worked for Jonye and for thousands of others...and I know it *will work for you*, too!

ACTION STEP

• Have you dropped your dream? Check the boxes below that apply to you.

• **Have you lost your dream for...**

    ❏ The salvation of your mate
    ❏ Your children to return to God
    ❏ Healing for yourself or a loved one
    ❏ To have your own ministry
    ❏ A better job
    ❏ Your own business
    ❏ Release from debt
    ❏ A better house or new car
    ❏ A loved one getting out of jail
    ❏ Other _____

• Now, put your hand on the list, and pray this prayer with me:

> *"Oh, precious, loving Lord forgive me for dropping my dreams. I repent of doubting You and the dreams You gave me. Please replant those dream seeds in my heart and renew the hope I have in you. Let Your will be done and Your dreams come true in my life. In Jesus' name. Amen."*

Chapter 7

⟫The Power To Prosper⟪
Through Partnership

Friend, today can mark the START OF NEW ANOINTINGS for some of the greatest days you've ever known thus far in your life!

In all my years of ministry, I have never seen or heard anything that comes close to what, I believe, God is preparing to do in this world through His children...men and women like you and me.

Yes! When you look at the news that is coming from the four corners of the world, you can clearly see that this could very well be the "Grand Finale" of the Holy Spirit's work before the return of Christ.

Do you long to see a flow of miracles in your own life and circumstances...and then an OVERFLOW to your children and children's children...even to your friends and loved ones?

I'm talking about miracles of healing, deliverance, triumph over tragedy, restoration from wrecked situations, miracles of abundance, and supernatural supply that are based on God's best from His storehouse!

The Lord has been directing us to intensify the

pace of ministry...increase the ranks of our partners... and prepare everyone to be a part of what God wants to do in these last days. DO YOU WANT TO BE A PART OF THAT?

If your answer is "Yes," then this could be your "divine appointment" to take a *step of faith* and get yourself into *partnership* with this ministry.

Paul's Philippian Partners

Paul the Apostle wrote several "partner letters" and one of them was to his ministry partners in Philippi. He says in chapter four verse 15-17, *"As you well know, when I first brought the Gospel to you and then went on my way...only you Philippians became my partners in giving and receiving. No other church did this. Even when I was over in Thessalonica you sent help twice. But though I appreciate your gifts, what makes me happiest is the well-earned REWARD YOU WILL HAVE because of your kindness"* (TLB).

Listen to me now—Christians all over the world quote Philippians 4:19,
"And my God shall supply all your need according to His riches in glory by Christ Jesus."
But they often miss the point. The people whose needs God is promising to supply are the people who are helping meet the needs of the ministry through *partnership* with His work.

As you partner to meet the needs of advancing the

gospel, God will partner with you to meet *your* needs *"...according to His riches in glory, because of what Christ Jesus has done for us."*

That's why Paul said, *"This makes me the happiest."* He was happy for his partners because he knew God would bless them with the same blessings that were taking place in his own ministry.

When you step into ministry partnership, you step into the MIRACLE ANOINTING of that ministry.

I believe every word I'm sharing with you about ministry partnership because I have personally experienced the awesome power that comes through it.

As I mentioned in the first chapter of this book, I remember the time when I became a ministry partner with Oral Roberts' ministry. History will show that Brother Roberts was one of the greatest healing evangelists, ministers, and Christian educators of the 20th century.

Dr. Oral Roberts has often said, "When you become partners with someone, the same *power of God* that's available to them becomes available to you—you literally walk in the same anointing they walk in!"

Do you know what happened when I became a partner with his ministry? I began to experience supernatural miracle manifestations of healing in my own meetings. Why? Partnership...ministry partnership. Because it's true: *When you become partners with someone, the same power of God that's available to them becomes available to you!*

There's a very real, very rich anointing that comes through ministry partnership. And this year, I want that anointing to be a "Miracle Overflow Generation Anointing"...something that would not only touch and bless you as a ministry partner, but we also desire to see it overflow to your children and grandchildren.

You can take your step of faith into the rewards, blessings, and anointing of ministry partnership today!

PRAYERFULLY CONSIDER BECOMING
A MONTHLY FAITH COVENANT PARTNER
WITH SARAH and ME.

End-Time Ministry

More than 25 years ago, God showed me that I needed partners to carry out His plan and vision for reaching the world with the Word. He told me that He would bring men and women together, like an army, to carry out His mission. He reminded me that He would not only anoint and bless the ministry, He also declared that He would anoint and bless each partner...as we shared the vision and the victory.

Yes! If ever there was a juncture in time when our heavenly Father wanted us to use everything at our disposal to spread the Word, that time is now.

There are *new end-time ministry doors* opening to us that up to now have been totally shut. The very same voices that used to shout *"No way!"* are now calling us and pleading and saying *"Any way* you can. Please come with your teaching from the Word."

We can't automatically say "Yes!" We can't go in with the Word and expand the ministry God has given us until He increases the ranks of the partners who will stand with us.

At the same time, the *very last thing* Satan wants to see you do is make a covenant decision of faith that can open the doors to greater blessings and miracles in you and your children's lives and circumstances.

When you become a partner with Sarah and me, I want you to know we become a partner with you, too, and we take it *very* seriously. It is a "covenant of faith" with both sides sharing the blessings and responsibilities.

OUR COMMITMENT TO YOU AS YOUR PARTNER...
This is what the Lord has prompted us to do:

FIRST: We want to send you a "Welcome Gift Package" designed exclusively for our Faith Covenant Partners...that recognizes and acknowledges your partnership with our ministry...and recognizes your commitment to help us fulfill the call God has given us to "COVER the EARTH With the WORD."

SECOND: Along with your "Welcome Gifts," we will make the following two-fold commitment of faith to you:

#1.) *To give you a "PARTNER PRAYER COVER"!* Sarah and I do our very best to personally pray for our partners every day...*without fail*...with special prayers of blessing. We often *"name" the day* [such as "victory day"] and declare that name to be our partners' banner of blessing for the day...and/or we prophesy over the day and speak a miracle word of faith for our partners [such as a "healing" word or "miracle supply" word] in whatever manner the Holy Spirit leads us that day.

Regardless of how the Lord directs our prayers, *every* day of the year...you will know in your heart...that a miracle prayer cover has been raised over you and your day by faith. We take this very seriously!

In addition to that...four times a year, we declare special days of prayer and fasting entirely for our partners and the prayer needs they send us.

#2.) *To equip and build your faith.* Sarah and I will send you additional (free) Partner Ministry/Helps Gifts, throughout the year. It could be a book, teaching cassette, or whatever the Lord directs and enables us to send you. It's also our way of sowing into your life as you remain faithful in partnership with us.

NOW IT'S YOUR TURN TO TAKE
THAT STEP OF FAITH.

Would you please consider becoming a Faith Covenant Partner with us in this ministry? We need your partner prayers and support like never before. But also, I believe you need the blessings that only God can bring to you by being a part of reaching out to the world through the power of partnership.

HOW DO YOU BECOME A PARTNER IN THIS MINISTRY?

You simply have to take a personal step of faith to do your best to do two things:

#1.) **Do your best** to pray for me, Sarah, and our ministry staff whenever the Holy Spirit quickens you to do so. Make us a part of your daily prayer pattern if you can. It's so important to keep this work surrounded and covered by prayer.

#2.) **Do your best** to give a regular monthly partner gift of support (of $20 or more), as the Lord enables you. There may be months you won't have it...other months you could have extra...just make the faith commitment to *do your best.*

Imagine—You can unleash the power of ministry partnership for less than the price of a cup of coffee...$20 dollars a month is about 65 cents a day.

Yes—you can supernaturally become a part of taking the Word around the world for less than what you would pay for a cup of coffee a day. That's really a small price to help feed the "Bread of Life" to tens of thousands daily.

AMBASSADOR AND CROWN AMBASSADOR PARTNERSHIP

An "Ambassador" partner is someone who pledges $100 a month or more. A "Crown Ambassador" pledges $1000 a month or more. Whichever way the Holy Spirit directs and enables you to make a monthly partner commitment, we would like to acknowledge your commitment level by sending additional ministry resource gifts—just for our Ambassador and Crown Ambassador partners.

I am praying that you will have enough faith and courage to say "yes" to the voice of God as He prompts you to join this ministry as a Faith Covenant Partner.

Make this a supernatural step of faith. Simply say,

"Heavenly Father—I want to enter into a new level of ANOINTING and BLESSING through the power of MINISTRY PARTNERSHIP! As I become a partner in Your work...I receive the same anointing that flows through this ministry...a miracle anointing that will overflow to everyone I touch; including my

*children and grandchildren. As You supply
my monthly commitment of partner support
[above my regular offerings]. I will be
faithful to give it (as a seed of faith)...and
I will be ready to reap the harvest that you
bring my way as You bless every seed I sow."*

Making Your Life Count

Yes, I believe ministry partnership is a step of faith that
you can't afford NOT to take. It's an investment that
reaps rich rewards in the kingdom of God as well as in
your life. Through partnership, you are making your life
count in greater ways than you ever could alone.

Look At This:

When you partner with this ministry...you are playing
an active part in God's work of teaching the Word every
day to hundreds of thousands of people all over the
world through this television outreach. You are helping
with miracle crusades that impact entire nations.

You are helping us to feed hungry children...clothe
orphans...train thousands of national pastors (all over
the world)...raise up and equip new ministers and
missionaries through our Word to the World College.
You are helping us distribute millions of pieces of
literature worldwide...and conduct Bible encounters
all over North America.

You are a partner in leading people to Christ and praying with hundreds every single day through our telephone ministry center...

...and the REWARDS, BLESSING, and ANOINTING of those efforts are passed on to you as a ministry partner by Christ Jesus.

REMEMBER: When you partner with a ministry, the same power of God that's available to that ministry becomes available to you—you literally walk in the same anointing they walk in!

GOD BLESS YOU and THANK YOU for making this a prayerful, personal decision.

 **ACTION STEP**

• PLEASE—regardless of what level you begin—just take the Partner Registration Request sheet at the end of this book, and mark the space that indicates your desire to become a "Faith Covenant Partner" with us.

• We'll rush your Welcome Package to you right away!

To order more copies
of this book
please see page 86 or 96.

Faith Covenant Partner Registration:

❏ "YES – I believe it's time for me to take advantage of the Miracle Benefits of Ministry Partnership. I want the very same anointing that rests upon your ministry to become available to me...to abide in my life and circumstances."

NAME (Mr. & Mrs. / Miss / Mr. / Mrs.) _____

ADDRESS _____

CITY _____ STATE/PROVINCE _____

ZIP/POSTAL CODE _____ COUNTRY _____

PHONE (H) ( ) _____

(W) ( ) _____

SIGNATURE

EMAIL _____
(Please include your email address so you can receive periodic updates.)

❏ I will pray for you and Sarah and the ministry as you continue "covering the earth with the Word."

❏ I am making a "standard" monthly Faith Promise of $30 (or more).
(62000/PA8X-MXXX)

❏ I would like to begin at a "higher" Faith Promise level of
$_____ per month. (62000/PA8X-MXXX)

❏ I would like to begin at the "AMBASSADOR" Partner Level with a Monthly Faith Promise of $100 or more per month. My Faith Promise will be
$_____ per month. (61000/PA8X-MXXX)

❏ I would like to begin at the "CROWN AMBASSADOR" Partner Level with a Monthly Faith Promise of $1000 or more per month. My Faith Promise will be
$_____ per month. (64000/PA8X-MXXX)

❏ AND I've enclosed my FIRST Faith Promise of $_____.

BANK CARD

O **Visa**   O **Mastercard**   O **Discover**   O **American Express**

Exp. Date _____

Card# _____

Amount of Your Gift/Donation $ _____

Name _____
(as it appears on card)

Signature _____

Phone ( ) - _____ - _____

THANK YOU & WELCOME! Your Partner "Welcome Gifts" will be automatically sent to you.

For additional copies of this book **OVER→**

Place this page in the postage-paid envelope provided and mail to:
Marilyn Hickey Ministries • P.O. Box 6598 • Englewood, CO 80155-6598

Keys to *More* Blessing

PRAYER REQUEST:

_____

_____

_____

_____

☐   I would like to order _____ additional copies of this book
"The Key to More MIRACLES in Your Life" at $4.95 each. (FPBK)

☐   I would like to sow $_____ as a seed into your ministry for
the miracle harvest I need.

☐   Please send me your FREE ministry magazine "OUTPOURING."

☐   **TOTAL AMOUNT ENCLOSED $_____**

NAME   Mr. & Mrs. / Miss / Mr. / Mrs.   _____

ADDRESS _____

CITY _____ STATE/PROVINCE _____

ZIP/POSTAL CODE _____ COUNTRY _____

PHONE   (H)   (   ) _____

(W)   (   ) _____

SIGNATURE _____

EMAIL_____

(Please include your email address so you can receive periodic updates.)

BANK CARD

○ **Visa**   ○ **Mastercard**   ○ **Discover**   ○ **American Express**

Exp. Date _____

Card# _____

Amount of Your Gift/Donation $ _____

Name _____

Signature _____
               (as it appears on card)

Phone (   ) - _____ - _____

Place this page in the postage-paid envelope provided and mail to:
Marilyn Hickey Ministries • P.O. Box 6598 • Englewood, CO 80115-6598

To become a PARTNER
◄—— **OVER**

mhmin.org

When you BECOME PARTNERS
with someone, the SAME POWER
of God that's available
to them becomes
available to you!

...See it **overflow**
to your **children**
& grandchildren!

The Lord is directing us to **intensify** the pace of ministry...

..as partners, we reach **across the world** with Encounters and crusades...

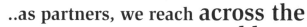

...Be a part of what God wants to do in these last days!

You need the multiplied blessings...

...that only **God can bring** to you by **being part** of **reaching out** to the world...

...through the **power of partnership.**

As a partner you help us...

...**feed** and clothe children, equip and **train** national **pastors** and missionaries, distribute the **gospel** and much more!

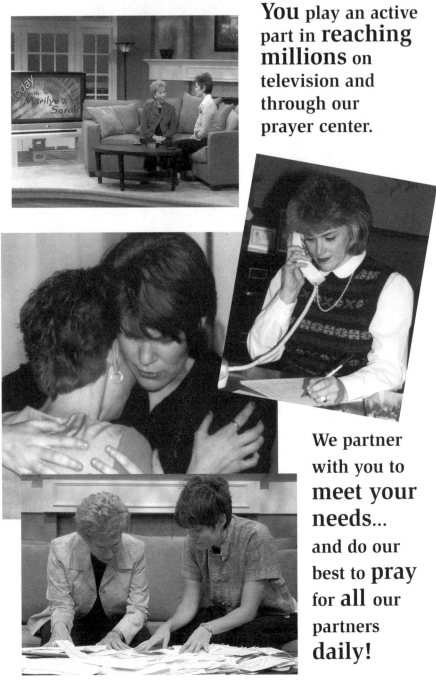

You play an active part in **reaching millions** on television and through our prayer center.

We partner with you to **meet your needs...** and do our best to **pray** for **all** our partners **daily!**

Make your life **count** by **partnering with us**

Faith Covenant Partner Registration:

❏ **"YES** – I believe it's time for me to take advantage of the Miracle Benefits of Ministry Partnership. I want the very same anointing that rests upon your ministry to become available to me...to abide in my life and circumstances."

NAME Mr. & Mrs. / Miss / Mr. / Mrs. _____

ADDRESS _____

CITY _____ STATE/PROVINCE _____

ZIP/POSTAL CODE _____ COUNTRY _____

PHONE (H) ( ) _____

(W) ( ) _____

SIGNATURE

EMAIL_____
(Please include your email address so you can receive periodic updates.)

❏ I will pray for you and Sarah and the ministry as you continue "covering the earth with the Word."

❏ I am making a "standard" monthly Faith Promise of $30 (or more).
(62000/PA8X-MXXX)

❏ I would like to begin at a "higher" Faith Promise level of
$_____ per month. (62000/PA8X-MXXX)

❏ I would like to begin at the "AMBASSADOR" Partner Level with a Monthly Faith Promise of $100 or more per month. My Faith Promise will be
$_____ per month. (61000/PA8X-MXXX)

❏ I would like to begin at the "CROWN AMBASSADOR" Partner Level with a Monthly Faith Promise of $1000 or more per month. My Faith Promise will be
$_____ per month. (64000/PA8X-MXXX)

❏ AND I've enclosed my FIRST Faith Promise of $_____.

B A N K   C A R D

O **Visa**   O **Mastercard**   O **Discover**   O **American Express**

Exp. Date _____

Card# _____

Amount of Your Gift/Donation $ _____

Name _____
(as it appears on card)

Signature _____

Phone ( ) - _____ - _____

THANK YOU & WELCOME! Your Partner "Welcome Gifts" will be automatically sent to you.

For additional copies of this book **OVER→**

Place this page in the postage-paid envelope provided and mail to:
Marilyn Hickey Ministries • P.O. Box 6598 • Englewood, CO 80155-6598

Keys to *More* Blessing

PRAYER REQUEST:

_____

_____

_____

_____

☐   I would like to order _____ additional copies of this book "The Key to More MIRACLES in Your Life" at $4.95 each. (FPBK)

☐   I would like to sow $_____ as a seed into your ministry for the miracle harvest I need.

☐   Please send me your FREE ministry magazine "OUTPOURING."

☐   **TOTAL AMOUNT ENCLOSED $_____**

NAME _____

ADDRESS _____

CITY _____ STATE/PROVINCE _____

ZIP/POSTAL CODE _____ COUNTRY _____

PHONE   (H)   (   ) _____

(W)   (   ) _____

SIGNATURE _____

EMAIL_____

(Please include your email address so you can receive periodic updates.)

BANK CARD

O **Visa**   O **Mastercard**   O **Discover**   O **American Express**

Exp. Date _____

Card# _____

Amount of Your Gift/Donation $ _____

Name _____

Signature _____
(as it appears on card)

Phone (   ) - _____ - _____

Place this page in the postage-paid envelope provided and mail to:
Marilyn Hickey Ministries • P.O. Box 6598 • Englewood, CO 80155-6598

To become a PARTNER
◄——— OVER

mhmin.org